Articulate as Rain

Articulate as Rain

Stephen Kampa

WAYWISER

First published in 2018 by

THE WAYWISER PRESS

Christmas Cottage, Church Enstone, Chipping Norton, Oxfordshire, OX7 4NN, UK
P.O. Box 6205, Baltimore, MD 21206, USA
https://waywiser-press.com

Editor-in-Chief
Philip Hoy

Senior American Editor
Joseph Harrison

Associate Editors
Eric McHenry | Dora Malech | V. Penelope Pelizzon | Clive Watkins
Greg Williamson | Matthew Yorke

Copyright © Stephen Kampa, 2018

9 7 5 3 1 2 4 6 8

A CIP catalogue record for this book is available from the British Library

ISBN 978-1-904130-91-8

Printed and bound by
T. J. International Ltd., Padstow, Cornwall, PL28 8RW

for John McComb

Acknowledgments

I am grateful to the editors and staff of the journals where these poems first found homes:

Able Muse: "God's Mnemonic," "Little, Late," "Total Discount, Total Savings"

Birmingham Poetry Review: "Dodo," "Nothing by Halves," "The Quiet Boy"

Chiron Review: "Couple Playing Catch"

Country Dog Review: "Skin Flicks"

The Cresset: "Something for Everything"

Dial 2: "Intellect Means Choosing Between"

First Things: "My Father's Father's Body," "Living Room Blues"

FLARE: The Flagler Review: "The Man Becomes the Music"

Hopkins Review: "Infinitives of Exile," "When I Don't Know What to Call This"

Measure: "Part Fear, Part Mourning, Part Wild Melody"

Poetry Northwest: "The Day James Schuyler Arrived," "Each Minute Rich with Infinite Potential," "Have It, Eat It"

Raintown Review: "'Tropical Cyclones Help to Maintain Equilibrium in the Earth's Troposphere, and to Maintain a Relatively Stable and Warm Temperature Worldwide'"

Rattle: "What He Must Have Seen"

The Same: "Walking on the Beach, I Keep Noticing a Sunbather"

Southwest Review: "Vehicle of Wonder"

Tampa Review: "Meant to Be"

32 Poems: "Meant, in Time, to Crack"

Unsplendid: "The Only Cure," "Reading Thomas Merton in *Le déjeuner des canotiers*"

Thanks to Don Selby and the *Poetry Daily* crew for reprinting "Meant, in Time, to Crack" and "Dodo." Thanks, as well, to Adam Vines, Richie Hofmann, and *Birmingham Poetry Review* for awarding poems published therein the Collins Prize.

Thanks to the fine folks at Waywiser, including Phil Hoy and Penelope Pelizzon, for useful feedback and for bringing this book to light. I'm especially grateful for the patience, graciousness, and editorial acumen of Joseph Harrison.

Friends and family: you remain crucial to the success of the operation. If I've thanked you before, I'm thanking you again. Eddie, Eric, and Jared: special thanks for all you do to make my life better.

Acknowledgments

Kristin: I can't think of the past seven years without uncommon gratitude for the way our friendship has deepened. I don't know what I would've done without you. Thank you. Thanks, too, to all my friends at Zen Bistro, where I have passed many pleasant hours thinking about poetry.

Thanks to friends at Flagler College, and especially Jay, Judith, and Kim; to friends at Embry-Riddle, and especially Jen, Michael, and Taylor; to my Hudson Valley friends Christina, Greg, and Todd; and to Nick Black, Billy Dean, Terrence Grayson, Victor Wainwright, and all the other musicians who ensured my few months in Memphis were memorable ones. Let's make music again soon.

Contents

Contents

4

There are not enough mouths to utter
all your fleeting names, O water.

— Wisława Szymborska

1

The Man Becomes the Music

It's not the saxophonist's fluent phrases
    Cascading in a silver chain
      Articulate as rain
    Unpetaling a bed of roses

That best conveys the tenor of our longing,
    But rather those thin, watery notes
      He breathlessly emotes
    As he runs out of air, still clinging

To the diluted hope death can't trump feeling
    (The way the last wet petal clings
      Fast to its bud, and swings
    In sputtering gusts, and flutters, falling).

"Tropical Cyclones Help to Maintain Equilibrium in the Earth's Troposphere, and to Maintain a Relatively Stable and Warm Temperature Worldwide"

—Wikipedia

Despite the forecast darkening the skies,
I down the sun tea I brewed yesterday
And head outside to mow the mangy lawn.
The mower wafts some gasolinish sighs
At first, coughs thickly, then gets underway.
I pace the yard like an automaton.

Last weekend's fallen branches crack like bones
Beneath the grinds and stutters of the mower,
And I imagine what the smallest thing
Out here endures as meteoric stones—
Blade-flung, enormous—soar into its lower
Realm, bringing what the heavens always bring.

Is it cartoonish to project the brittle
Notions my shredded crickets might have held
Or to infer what fire ants, brutally caught,
Felt as the whirling fury of my little
One-cylinder, gas-powered, hand-propelled
Climate became for them a final thought?

Break time. The Weather Channel in my brisk
Den swims with news. A three-piece suit is tracing
A hurricane's track through the Everglades.
The animated storm is a rough gray disk;
My state's lacustrine eye stares, as if facing
The swiftest and most purposeful of blades.

The Day James Schuyler Arrived

The serious gray
rain kept me
indoors today
the way a lover
keeps one in
bed. I drank
good smoked
teas, I read good
poems in praise
of apple cores
and peonies—
read, too, some
bad ones. I took
three hot showers
without feeling
much cleaner.
Today, like most
days, I wanted
to feel like part
of something,
but mostly I was
a part of books:
the crackle of
one's first being
opened, the light
mulchy smell
of fresh pages.
Now I'm listening
to Art Blakey,
whose brushwork
lisps like washes
of wind-lashed
rain against wet
leaves punctuated
by syncopated
rim shots that

knock like gust
flung acorns
against a roof,
I'm sipping crisp
amber ale and
silently chanting,
Au revoir, arete!
The only thing
I did today was
today: mercifully
remiss, I hovered,
stalled, savored
the damp cool
of my apartment,
and if I caused
myself or God—
the God I barely
spoke to today—
any pain, I can
only offer this
muted pleasure:
tonight I changed
my sheets from
purple to gray in
honor of the rain.

Little, Late

How many nights has something close
    To happiness brushed past
The way a stranger threads a bar
    And shoulders by so fast
He knocks you clockwise, dumps your drink,
    Yet never checks his pace,
Failing to catch your muttered threats
    Or glimpse your mottled face?

Much later, bottles deep, you'll stumble
    On just the words, a fit
(Though canned) expression—one more classic
    Case of beer-case wit—
And as you blear your way through comebacks,
    You'll feel your stomach clench
For points you'd score if you just had
    His number and more French.

I've known those nights—as well as any,
    As if I'd written them—
And others, too, where down some alley
    A restless requiem
Came humming, bar by bar, from shadows
    Where water drops like clocks
Kept measuring the falling seconds
    That followed me for blocks,

And others still where something close
    To happiness would dawdle
At darkened doors or, parked for hours,
    Would open up the throttle
And peel away in smoke, and much as
    My paeans to despair
Came naturally, I came to trade
    Those poems for a prayer:

That happiness, just once, would stop
    And shock me with a look
So sad and scarred I'd pardon it
    For all the time it took
To find me. Well. I couldn't tell you
    During which water drop
I hardened past the point of hoping
    That happiness would stop,

But one night, home alone, exhausted
    By all the rot and rote,
I heard it humming one room over
    And knew by one low note
That it had come for me at last—
    Knew, too, the antidote.
The ice in my glass cracked its knuckles.
    The whiskey cleared my throat.

What I Learned Drinking Away My Sorrows

No matter
how many
hundred-
proof bottles
I've zeroed
and belittled
with not a
little sway

and slur to blur
my winning
words while
I stagger
off, slip away—
no matter
how many
wet bursts

of week it
takes to see
spirits fall
like a fund-raiser
thermometer
working in
reverse, a
sure measure

of both cool
air and how
much less
I've come to
care—I'll come
to pour
that bottom
finger's worth

of whiskey
into my glass
(just kill it
already, it'll
be your last
drink), and when
I do, I fill it,
and know then

I'll have to
learn the burn-
ing lesson
again, that at
that last sip
at the very
brink, there is
always, *always,*

more than you think.

Soon to Be Twice a Week

These garbage cans deployed in neat
Rows by their driveways look as serious,
Straight-backed, and silently imperious
As soldiers on a conquered street.

Total Discount, Total Savings

I buy my paper cups and paper plates
In bulk while, nearby, bleary beggars shake
And know the hunger nothing satiates—

Their disappointment never dissipates.
I feel for them, whatever their mistake.
I buy my paper cups and paper plates

And pray for faceless poverty, the spates
Undone by indolence who wake and bake
And know the hunger nothing satiates.

Some pliable statistic indicates
A buck a day saves lives: give me a break.
I buy my paper cups and paper plates

Just the same. The government inflates
Those counts of bums who booze for boozing's sake
And know the hunger nothing satiates,

And I don't buy them. No one allocates
My wallet. Some of us have lives to make.
I buy my paper cups and paper plates
And know the hunger nothing satiates.

Skin Flicks

In this one, the woman dressed like a nurse comes
    home with vomit on her uniform;
her husband slumps over the kitchen table,
    bills spread out like a jigsaw puzzle;
they'll argue, scatter sheets, slam doors. In this one,
    the woman with large, pendulous breasts
will miscarry, and you will see an extreme
    close-up of the bloody toilet bowl;
she'd already bought child-resistant covers
    for all the electrical outlets
and a safety gate for the staircase. In this
    one, teens in tiny bikinis rub
in the fat, one-piece girl's failure: they call her
    Dorkimedes, tell her not to dive
in unless she wants to displace the whole damn
    ocean, ask her if she had a whale
of a time or a whale for breakfast; and you
    and I will watch the whole thing. In this
last one, we will stare as a breathtaking young
    mother catches her daughter playing
connect the dots with her grandma's liver spots
    during those final unconscious hours
in the hospital, and the mother will slap
    this daughter so hard across the face
that a red spot forms on her cheek, its carmine
    recrimination the final dot
to connect in the picture we are forming.
    Now the skin flicks end; the lights go on.
I'm sorry: you came here looking for the nurse
    fetish's most perfect expression,
for schoolgirl skirts and French maid fishnet stockings;
    for jumbo jugs and titanic tits,
for barely legal filmed-on-her-birthday teens,
    for MILFs and goth chicks and girls next door,

butt-spelunkers, deep-throat queens, and coldcocked sluts;
   and you have been given this instead.
All you wanted was to see some skin. You did.
   Spend the day in it. Here are your shoes.

Immaterial Witness

How badly we need the robot cellphones sprouting legs
and climbing up
                  our arms to drill their holes through our skulls,
the effete bespectacled doc hardwiring a brain
to car batteries, mechanisms and mechanics,
the world of nutrients
                  and gunshot wounds, to believe
anything is happening to us.
                        If I tell you

a man is injecting a banned chemical substance
into the soft
                  neck of a demoiselle so she'll grow
as pliable as a hunk of bread dough, you'll Google
the National Guard, but when I tell you they use bold
primary colors in
                  fast food joints to connect them
to early childhood toys, or that one
                        luxury car

manufacturer targets advertising at kids
six years old so
                  by the time it's time to buy one, the man
walking into the dealership has had two decades
of skits and jingles convincing him he's decided
on this model on his
                  own, you'll tell me to get real,
get out, get along, that's just business
                        or none of mine,

get tough, going, lucky, smart, get while the getting's good,
get a clue, get
                    a life. We need the pale electrode
pads like strange white flowers, we need the quantum-powered
neuronanobots, we even need the cold comfort
of the apocryphal
                    Coca-Cola flash frame ad,
even if only for a fraction
                              of a second

at think-proof speeds that make it impossible to see
without freezing,
                    we need the high-tech mind-control pen
and not the psych studies on orange ink, we need the love
potion of pheromone scratch 'n' sniff stickers and not
experts talking dirty
                    lingerie lists, and we need
not admit we let our pleasure in
                              sex cues excuse

our inadvertent desire: we *want* to be rum-primed.
As for God's grace,
                    we never believed a word of it.
We find the immaterial immaterial.
We're people people, we like to put names to faces
and never place a verb
                    before a noun. As for terms
and bargains, we hold our ends up once
                              we've nailed them down.

Intellect Means Choosing Between

Unsold on any afterlife,
    Unmoved by thoughts of will,
You've started celebrating nature's
    Aleatory skill
As manifest in, first and foremost,
    You and your family,
Genus, and species, but also in
    The famous profligacy
Of beetles or the useful hodgepodge
    Of hedgehog quills, squid ink,
And wasp nests shaped from proto-paper;
    At times, you almost think

This mindless cosmic conversation
    Knit of genetic patter
Bespeaks a pattern too contrived
    For matter not to matter—
Substance has substance, you might say—
    And you suspect the drift
Of tides (both nucleo- and not)
    Betrays an unlikely gift;
Amazed by the gut-retching sea
    Cucumber, anglerfish
Dangling bright lures, oceans awash
    With awe, you almost wish

(If neurochemistry and chains of
    Said cause to said effect
Could be so called) you could express
    How fine your intellect
Finds chaos grown to cosmic gambol;
    And, almost moved to praise,
You wonder whom you'd give the credit,
    Uncertain how to phrase

Such unobjective gratitude.
You think, you thank—almost—
Then choose to give it up to chance,
Of which you have no ghost.

Devil Got My Number

I hear the devil laughing every time
I challenge him to one more longshot match
And—cocksure of a bull's-eye, feeling prime—
I still come up with scratch,

Another goose egg on the scoreboard lit
With lifetime stats where rows of zeroes gain
This latest brilliant *oh*, a cinch to fit
Onto their golden chain.

The devil's got my number, got it good,
And not because he chanced a gutsy guess
During a stakeout in my neighborhood
And knocked at my address,

Nor because some ex-chit of mine divulged
My digits, part of a payback binge one night;
I met no carny who, as my eyes bulged,
Bluffed out of me my height

Or weight, I.Q. or age, no well-disguised
Tailor who stole my inseam measurements,
No bookworm who perused my new revised
Table of discontents

To find the page on which my final breaking
Point's codified, plus which size bits will chafe;
I caught no faceless shadow tasked with taking
The passcode to my safe;

Nor is it any matter of gematria
Translating me to math, nor of some call
To swell the random lockstep ranks pro patria—
It's not like that at all.

It's more like he's been jostling in a line,
Counting his change as the crowd begins to thicken
And thinking to himself, *It's all divine,*
This time I'll have the chicken,

And bone-hungry, half-starved, he's holding steady,
He's creeping forward, flipping a brand-new quarter,
He's standing at the counter, and he's ready
To place his usual order.

God's Mnemonic

The beauty we've forgotten stays forgotten
In heaven, too, unmemorable, unmissed;
By contrast, our disfigurements persist
Like igneous rocks or an eternal thought in

The mind of God: the palsied lurch and stumble,
Outgrowths and fleshy gaps from the atomic
Fallout, wet empty sockets, the semi-comic
Hydrocephalic bulge—they keep us humble,

More down-to-earth, distinctly kind, and should
No more define perdition than election.
Why think affliction must preclude affection?
Why think our earthly horrors bring no good

News of their own? It's time that we confess
With every awful blemish, every chronic
Eruption or collapse, the oldest chthonic
Law becomes clear: through our unsightliness,

We grow more recognizable from afar.
Perhaps God tires of beauty's cool, laconic
Demeanor. Perhaps pain is God's mnemonic:
We scar so he'll remember who we are.

Omniscience: Omnipathy

An expert at exceptions, you would play with
Your mother's favorite necklace while you thrilled
To afternoon cartoons—you were quite skilled
At gauging what a kid could get away with—
And as you watched, a nervy porcupine
Would grab a branch and jury-rig a bow,
Pull out some quills, and fire a whistling row
Of whimpers at some hound dog down the line.

Your impulse was to cover up your eyes;
Your fingers made a little fleshly cage.
Your tolerance got better with your age,
And, as a teen, although you'd sympathize
With Candy, soon to feel the chainsaw's kiss,
You only sometimes left for popcorn when
The chainsaw's teeth went grinding through her skin,
And you'd come back to catch the last of Kris.

Later you graduated to the good
Stuff: takeout General Tso's, a glass of red,
A sweet romantic comedy in bed
Beside a woman who, you understood,
Cherished you more than any heroine
Hollywood could devise. On nights the plot
Grew far too tangled ever to unknot,
You stopped the movie and let love begin,

Unwilling to keep watching as the leads
Misspoke, mishandled missed cues, and misstepped
Till, at their wits' and screenplay's end, they wept
Tears as perfectly formed as small glass beads;
And one such night, your daughter first took shape—
High laughter, curls, a face she'll try to bury
Deep in couch cushions when it gets too scary
To watch her cartoon field mouse mid-escape.

Now when you turn the television on,
It channels your apocalyptic fears.
A woman on the news distills to tears
As she describes her kidnapped daughter, gone
For eighteen days; a student tries to hurl
Bricks at a row of stenciled barricades;
Police investigate three bombed parades,
Each in a different state; they find the girl;

And when you think it can't grow more obscene
(It's both unbearable and the same old thing),
A man is brought to trial for necklacing,
Which means he drenched a tire with gasoline—
A tire he'd forced around some boy—and set it
On fire, then watched. The smoke was dark and thick.
The still shot of the victim made you sick:
So much burned meat. You've prayed you might forget it.

You turn your widescreen off, but you're surrounded
By all the sorry eyesores of your life:
Your daughter has been feuding with your wife
And last night during dinner had astounded
You both by jamming fingers in her ears
And trilling nonsense syllables to drown
The conversation out, and you'd put down
Your fork and knife, spit out your half-chewed spears

Of dank asparagus, and loosed a word
That made both women jerk back from the table.
You sulked and peeled off a beer bottle label
Like dead skin from a blister. Evening blurred
To morning—now, today—the day you visit
Your mother in the wing for memory care,
A horrid place (you hardly see her there),
And yes, you know, the irony is exquisite,

Given that one way she would punish you
Was with a timeout, where you had to sit
Alone and contemplate whatever bit
Of devilry you'd learned you shouldn't do.
Of that, no end: the quarrels, cracks, white lies,
The eagerness to slip a filthy joke in,
The budget shortfall fixed, the faith long broken—
Your impulse is to cover up your eyes,

To hide these from yourself as children hide
Links from a broken necklace in a jar,
Forgetting, once they're hidden, where they are.
You need fresh air. You take a stroll outside,
And looking up, perhaps you long to say,
"The skies declare the glory of the Lord."
Elsewhere, a man untarps a waterboard.
Pity the God who cannot look away.

Have It, Eat It

What I expect
to see at the end
   isn't the moon
gray as a dusty plate
   or red as
a party balloon let go

   because its holder
just couldn't wait to open
   her first gift,
tearing sky-blue paper the way
   the sky itself
will be torn to celebrate

   in due time
with apt atmospherics the day
   we all were
born, nor dune upon dune
   of radioactive sand
blowing in a staticky hiss

   like a radio
tuned to all the news
   we'll miss once
the party's over and everyone's
   gone, but this:
one bare, branchless tree, straight

   as the barrel
of an enormous gun, stuck
   like a toothpick
in the cakey, sun-warmed mud
   to see if
finally the world is done.

2

The Quiet Boy

The talk turned, as it always did, to power,
Or more precisely, to the superpowers
The boys would die for. All of them were boys.

They camped out in the corner of the band room
During lunch hours that felt too long for them,
Extracting chips and Cheetos from their bags

While they discussed telepathy, time travel,
Teleportation, and the finer points
Of flight: "Of course it's badass," said the one

Who said most everything as if he knew
Most everything, "but you can go too high,
And then what?" Here he hammed it up: gasps, gurgles.

"Can't breathe. You pass out. Then you better hope
You turn invincible before you land."
He crunched his Bugle with authority.

"Pyrokinesis," purred the lone bold boy
Who dared to smoke. "Oh, please," another countered,
"Hydrokinesis. Since we're mostly water."

"Invisibility," daydreamed the boy
With acne so persistent and intense—
His face pink, amber-grainy, strafed with strips

Of peeling skin—he seemed a poorly made
Piñata, "I'd pick that one. Just imagine
The things you'd see!" The boys all paused then, lost

In puffs and pallors none of them had seen
Except online. One wiped his salty fingers
Across his jeans. Another gulped his Crush.

The quiet boy, as usual, said nothing.
Invisibility? Dumb. Just plain dumb.
Why choose a power you already had?

Dodo

Standing before his boss, his clipboard clutched
Tightly against his chest as though it might be
The breastplate of some long-outdated suit
Of armor, strangely small and thin, he listens
While from the howling suckhole of a face

He's recently begun to recognize
In dreams, whole gales of imprecation swell
The room, balloon it, till the walls themselves
Seem stretched, tensed, straining not to fly apart
While words as imprecise as musket balls

Go burring through the air. He tells himself,
Nothing can touch me, nothing in the world
Can move me, centers, breathes the three deep breaths
He's read about in books by Buddhist monks,
And stares above and slightly to the left

Of all that raddled, gaping, goggle-eyed
Absurdity and at a beautiful
Framed watercolor of a famous dodo,
Its head shaped wrong, its rump ridiculous,
The bulge where neck meets body most suggestive

Of some unswallowable morsel caught
Bone-like between its beak and tufty gut,
And nearly all its feathers slate blue-gray
Except for golden sun-flares on the wings
That dangle at its sides, unflappable.

Couple Playing Catch

Their baseball gloves' oiled leather scents can't reach me,
But they don't need to; I remember them
From when I played. I'm in a park. A man
Punches his glove and shouts, "Let's see that arm!"

I can remember many things: the white
Price tag that dangled flag-like in surrender,
Thick rubber bands that helped to shape the pocket,
The satisfying smack of caught pop flies,

The clean white chalk of baselines. The woman throws,
And the ball dribbles to a grassy stop
Inches away from the man's outstretched glove.
Metal bats pinging, the taste of Gatorade,

Books about yetis and the Loch Ness Monster,
Books about dinosaurs—I read them days
The coach would bench me. I can smell the leather
The way a paleobiologist

Can brush millennia of mesa dust
From a wing bone and an archaeopteryx
Lifts off in flight, the way loch-watchers know
Ripples mean life below. "You throw like a girl!"

"Grow up!" the woman says, as if he couldn't,
Or if not up, then old, like everyone.
I try but can't imagine cavemen playing
Baseball, or stickball, things with sticks and stones.

I wonder: was it simply our survival
Skills could be honed by playing games like these?
Why else devise them? "Come on, put some sting
On it!" the man exclaims, and she lets go

A hissing pitch that pops him in the nose.
It bleeds. "Oh, God!" he cries. "I think you broke it!"
I would believe in leisure, or in pleasure,
And in the distant past find happiness

Were that a mercy time could still bestow;
But for a moment, in their game, I'm shown
Two worlds at once, an epochs-old tableau—
The charging boar, the thrown primordial stone.

Living Room Blues

I feel less lonely when I watch TV:
The heartbreak and the healing both go quicker,

And Marketing's best minds keep courting me
As though my name were capping a marquee—

It might as well, since I control the clicker.
I feel less blue, too, watching: though TV

Can't do much more than mute a tragedy
(The ten o'clock news scrolls its frantic ticker),

It compensates with ample comedy—
Reruns alone could last an eternity!

That comfort bathes me in its bluish flicker.
I feel less lonely when I watch TV,

Though lately not as often. When I see
My favorite sitcom couples snipe and bicker—

They used to smile, to *beam*, accepting me
Into their homes; now they seem less carefree,

And the canned laughter sounds like one long snicker.
I get so lonely when I watch TV,

Where everyone plays a part apart from me.

Infinitives of Exile

To feel the toilet seat's cool ass-kiss, tear
Through gauzy sheets of single-ply, and wipe
Only to overfill this stranger's toilet
And scramble for the plunger while the water
Brims past the porcelain lip and pours across
The floor you now discover is uneven
Until it seeps beneath the bathroom door
And down the hall; to court insomnia
In beds too hard or soft, too short or narrow,
In bedrooms lacking locks or decent lighting
In houses where your sexual ambitions
Are sure to wilt like poorly potted ferns
Parched in a dirt as dry as the forgotten
Meatloaf your hostess meted out with shy
Smiles of apology; or to cavort
In boxer shorts around the empty house
(At last the owners, in a show of trust,
Have gone to try some local theater),
To yodel through the kitchen while performing
Your most emphatic pelvic thrusts of joy,
The wildest hip gyrations in your secret
Yet quite distinctly large Gyrepetoire,
Until you see your hosts, who left their keys
In plain sight on a living room end table,
Staring at you—no, more precisely, staring
With unadulterated awestruck horror
Down at your crotch, where you discover, first,
Your boxer-button has unfastened, leaving
An ample aperture for, second, one
Enormously embarrassing erection . . .

To find your mild discomforts or your major
Humiliations honed or ground to nothing
By the grit-stippled edge of gratitude,
The gratitude you owe and know you owe,
Given your exile, to those who take you in,

Is to remember even in your body
You are a guest, at times a tawdry one:
How many weekends have you soaked your liver
In single-malt conviviality,
How often do you boot up your machine
And double-click on a solitary life
Closely resembling low-grade catatonia?
Not the best guest behavior, you'd admit,
And one more reason you can't stay forever.
And if foreshadowing suggests a time
Your exile will require you leave your body,
Well, you already knew that; worse than this
Will be your exile from your *life*, that story
You tell yourself in misremembered fragments
And flattering light—others will prove the authors
After you've gone, and they'll remember you
As they see fit. Perhaps your tale will take on
Mythic proportions—though, more likely, nothing
Will make your story's probable distortions
More than the humdrum ones—but rest assured
Whatever happens, you will only be
A visitor to that life, someone who signed,
In ink that glistened then without a trace
Of fading on the crisp, unyellowed pages,
A guestbook in a slant, old-timey hand.

What He Must Have Seen

He's so old that a man has to stand on either side of him
to prop him up, but he gangles there on his own legs, climbing
the stairs slowly to the baptistery where the pastor waits,

youthful and brimming with a swift, practiced benevolence now
that the old codger has finally made up his mind for Christ,
and the man totters on the concrete edge of the pool before

he tremor-steps sideways down yet more stairs into the water,
where the standard words are spoken, and he goes under but can't
come up by himself, so the two attendant men are rushing

over to help the pastor haul him to the surface, the prayer
gets said, a little orotund still despite the breathlessness
tugging at the pastor's voice, then we watch the slow ascension

out of the water, and here the sopping man can't hold himself
upright anymore, he has to put his hands down on the stairs
to steady himself, the other men surrounding him, their hands

at his scabbed, purplish elbows or against the small of his back
while we the congregation hold our one long bored breath, praying
that he won't slip and fall, crack open his spotty pate and bleed

into the baptistery, and I think he must have seen this
the moment he decided to be baptized, he must have known
that he would have to clutch arms and rails and even the black edge

of the piano to help himself be hoisted out, and all
in front of this smarts-riddled crowd come of age in the age of
the body, the youthful body, the digital blink, the why

is he taking so long to get out, knew he would have to put
one knee on a step, a hand, another knee, another hand,
up and up, over and over, and he chose it, chose this path

we raced past, our pose his posture, our figures of speech his facts
as he crawls, in front of God and everybody, as he crawls
on his hands and knees into a new life, short but eternal.

Where You Were Going

Here I am at another open mike that opened
with Bob Seeger, the zillionth time I've heard those pages
turned inexpertly, intently, and I'm wondering
how best to measure out my life: morning and evening
are taken and too much alike, the sun coming up
or going down, it's all the same rotation, the hours
like swift similes in a more important passage,
and Eliot's coffee spoons are out, ditto the leaves
with their color-coded prerecorded messages,
so it comes down to the bars—the twelve I've been playing
since I began playing, the I-IV-V familiar
as certain verses from the Bible, or the raised ones
I'll never get even one leg over, or the one
Tennyson had to cross, and did, for lack of options,
or the bars I've whiled away my time in, a timeout
from the helter-skelter imperatives of higher
education and higher callings because sometimes,
yeah, baby, we all wanna get low down, way down low.
Count them: the plastic ashtrays and splashy cymbal fills,
the melodies composed entirely of quarter
notes, the back walls composed entirely of beer cans,
the Drifters tunes and cold drafts and rough drafts I've scribbled
in the neon benevolence of bar lights while harsh
sibilants snip through the air and glasses contribute
their accents in accidents of emphasis, faceless
waiters and flotillas of bewitching bartenders,
microphones and microbrews, the sudden clipped feedback
from inebriated patrons and hot monitors—
why should these be any worse than turgid liturgies
spacing out the tame Sundays I spent time spacing out,
than the wrinkled, rankled lines of homeless goobers fed
on Friday nights by tireless, dateless do-gooders?
Worse than the annual booze cruise or semimonthly
minge binge, worse than the nightly pint of Ben and Jerry's
over one more rerun marathon featuring thin
attractive people chasing thin attractive people?

How are these pained escapades any better than mine
as temporal punctuation? I'd argue they aren't,
I'd swear that they're all equally the revelations
of rhythm, torn pages separating days from days,
weeks from weeks, and of them, there can never be enough:
the televised games, the playlists, the lame trivia,
the AA batteries, the bottle caps, the coils
of Monster cables, power ballads and power chords,
the nickel-plated disappointments, the unending
renditions of "Before You Accuse Me," the broken
strings, the broken ties, the bluely illuminated
glasses hanging from wooden racks, the crumbling corks,
the crumpled napkins, the crack of pool balls, the poohbahs
laying claim to intimate knowledge of the hottest
waitress, pentatonic runs and runs in pantyhose,
the weeks of cooking grease and epochs of Styrofoam—
the blue-collar mystics all assert the sacrament
of the present moment, and all in all, who isn't
in need of sacraments? Interminable mornings
of data entry dissolve to interminable
afternoons of data entry. Radio singles
pace the background and, keen to save us, keep sugaring
the air. Maybe you look forward to a ritzy lunch
at an upscale uptown bistro; maybe you'd settle
for meeting a potential mate without a MeGram
shrine dedicated to hordes of half-naked duckface
selfies. You know that life requires more intensity
before it will become clear the way sand requires heat
and pressure before it will become glass. You'll chuckle
at the few clever commercials that prank the airwaves;
you'll resist punching the owners of shit pickup trucks
with bumper stickers that read The Obama Nation
is an Abomination; you'll abandon small talk
as a means of making work feel less like being rolled
down a hillside covered with soot and old cutlery.
Locks will rust shut, pearl buttons will pop from your valiant

if overcommitted sleeves, and during your brief Zen
phase, you'll decide this means open and closed have become
the same thing. You'll spend inordinate amounts of time
making irrelevant decisions: detergent brands,
the color of your sweatpants, whether to watch the film
with the graphic violence or the graphic nudity,
honeymoon spots. You'll collect souvenir shot glasses
and, with help from myrmidonian friends, propagate
a personal mythology regarding your car.
Sometimes, half gone, you'll imagine there are secret codes
woven into the gold stitching on a pair of jeans
or convince yourself that your hair's so sexy-messy
everyone in the bar wants to bang you sidesaddle,
but mostly you'll blanch with anger when a waiter brings
you ranch or honey mustard instead of barbecue
sauce for dipping your chicken tenders, and you'll wonder
which of the infinite variables in this cold
cause-and-effect cosmos predisposed you to flashes
of rage: DNA, parental disputes, the wrong book?
Occasionally you'll envy a man or woman
with bleachier teeth or more notable hair, but soon
enough you'll enter your spiritually mature
phase, as you like to call it—all the time, when speaking
to anyone—wherein you'll take clamorous delight
in quotidiana: a cute toddler will mangle
a simple word, the events of the day will balance
in pleasing symmetries, and you'll dial up your aura,
suspecting your delectation of these minutiae
bespeaks the broadness, even the largesse, of your soul.
When you finally realize you've been ignoring
your practice of leaving indelicately small tips,
the plain relish with which you imagine targeting
a person's ugliest physiognomic feature
and informing her of it, your habit of saying
you when you mean *I* and *I* when you mean *everyone,*
you'll have come close enough to enlightenment to know

that enlightenment was only going to take you
so far—maybe this far—anyway. You are old now:
the unknown country is awaiting you. Your whole life
takes as its context that imminent trip. Most of it
has begun to sound like a synopsis preceding
a more vital story. Why, then, would the phone numbers
on pens matter? The real ingredients of the first
Singapore sling? The inadvertence of a local
ad with its ill-advised slogan for a sealcoating
specialist: "LET ME FILL UR CRACKS"? Your ability
to improvise dirty lyrics to any '80s
pop song? The deepest umbrage of your adolescence?
I can define mercy: it's suddenly no longer
wishing your life had been other than it was. You feel
about it the way you sometimes feel about your first
car: sure, it wasn't a car, exactly, but instead
a sports van older than you were, as scabbed and rusted
as disused playground equipment, and yes, it sported
an eight-track player and—I shit you not—white curtains
in all the windows, and maybe the brakes did give out
on your way to the airport to pick up your girlfriend,
the one you haven't been able to talk to in years,
and admittedly it had shag carpet on the floor
and ceiling, which made your pastor call it The Sin Bin
and suggest a bumper sticker that said IF THE HOUSE
IS ROCKIN', DON'T BOTHER KNOCKIN', and when it was all
sad and done, driven past distraction to destruction,
sure, you had to leave it roadside in another state,
but it was yours, and it got you where you were going.

Sleeve Tattoos

Scales? Feathers? Spider webs? The intricate
Arm's-length abstractions of a mandala,
Elaborations of a labyrinth?

From back here—corner table, near the darts—
It's hard to see the pattern, but they cover
His arms in bredes of phosphorescent blue.

His sleeveless t-shirt brings to mind a jerkin.
Chainmail? Medusan hair? An ourobouros?
Perhaps most frightening of all: fine print?

Whatever else they mean, they mean he's safe
From nakedness. I want to ask him how
He chose the things about himself he thought

Would never change, whether they have already,
But then impermanence is my obsession.
Maybe it's more the images chose him

For pinpoint presentations of the truth
That everyone must learn unless death comes
Too soon, that something—name it what you will:

Fate, physics, circumstances, God—will pierce you
More times than you can count, over and over
Ad astra, prick by prick and scar by scar,

Staining you with its bright designs on you.
No matter how they fade, the way you fit
That picture is, at long last, who you are.

3

The Explanation

I'd almost managed to convince myself
Someday we'd kiss, or at least hold hands as we strolled along a lakeside
And fumbled toward our feelings, but I know
Nothing like that will obtain: poor daydreams, the lot of them, unlikely
And strikingly unlovely in their greed.
Friendships enrich us as much, last longer than even great romances,
And work as well as cleanly written prose.
Why would I gamble on love? Some thousands of feet beneath the ocean,
A diver finds a chest. He knows already
Something invaluable lies there, padlocked and waterlogged, but priceless.
He ought to haul it up and crack it open,
Start the delicious account—groats, ducats, doubloons, a palm-sized diamond,
A compass as ornate as any broach,
Maps for a world that the world grew out of an age ago, yet didn't,
And sapphires that become, for just a moment,
Bright and inedible glass blueberries—but something else detains him:
A little further down, a little deeper,
Tilted uncannily, some rust-covered protrusion—like a doorknob—
Arises from the seabed, and the diver
Knows it's unlikely that here, half-buried, unsought, may lie the entrance
Into that unimaginable city
Lost for millennia, *knows* it, yet swears he can see the doorknob turning.

We Have Agreed

More happy love! more happy, happy love!

— Keats

We have agreed to be
More friends than lovers. *This is no one's fault,*
We tell ourselves with feigned serenity,
    Accepting what we say.
    We have agreed the way
The ocean has agreed to hold less salt.

We also have a greed
For more: more love, more loving, loveliness
We'd squeeze from every hour at every speed.
    Our sheet-enshrined caresses
    And soft, concerted yesses
Are touchy subjects, trying to redress,

But since we have agreed—
As wind and water do, as light and shade—
That we are friends, to friendship we concede,
    Although what is most striking
    Is that, to neither's liking,
We can't lie in the bed we haven't made.

The ocean in its bed
Furrows its brow with every wave. Heart-sinking.
Through panoplies of clouds piled overhead,
    The stars tonight look faultless.
    That selfsame ocean—saltless,
Fresh as fresh rain—is what we can't stop drinking.

Took All These Years

As every sculptor must
Sift absent marble dust,
And every painter stare
Down the masterpiece
That isn't there,

And every dancer feel
Stone-like beneath his heel
The step on which he stumbled,
And every orator mouth
The word he mumbled,

And every tenor hear
Haunting his inner ear
The note he couldn't hit,
We all relive one love,
And ours was it,

Elizabeth. By chance
Tonight I caught a glance
Of you, a recent post
That blazed into my bed-
room like a ghost

And crackled in my hand,
A phoned-in reprimand
From someone who's moved on
And, in that far light, seems
Glad to be gone.

Do you remember dinner
One autumn in the inner
Loop in Chicago where
You panted and unpinned
Your sweaty hair,

Letting it fall in swoops
Of sparked light, golden loops,
Before that moment when
You'd cooled enough to pin it
Back up again?

Lost in the now spellbinding
Replaying and rewinding
Of that last scene, I sigh
And realize how much
Escaped my eye—

Such dated knowledge stings—
Though of the many things
Missed in my misappraisal,
One detail stands out most:
Your eyes are hazel,

And in this pic he took—
The one in which you look
At him outside the frame—
I recognize a light
I now could name

And know a keener man,
Rightly enamored, can
Night after night devote his
Kisses to all the graces
I didn't notice.

What can I do? I sing,
Since all I have to bring
In answer to that light
Are the few lines that, once,
I failed to write.

Event Horizon

Your bruises look worse today,
　　less pear brown-yellow
than stormy muscadine. You say
　　you don't know
how they got that way,
　　they looked just

fine this morning, but this
　　afternoon I squeezed
your arm right where, joy-ridden,
　　I invariably do
before I kneaded your hips
　　and drew you

down further, pressing you flat
　　against my chest.
It might have been that.
　　Now we're talking
about the rest, the complications
　　love always invites

since it can't always be
　　love-bruises and love-bites:
the two jobs, our estranged
　　beliefs, certain gray
areas (your husband, your son),
　　whether this would

ever work anyway and what
　　it would mean
if it were suddenly done.
　　We're thinking it
might be best to take
　　some time rather

than a shot. Meanwhile, desire
   galaxies your arm,
darkening, deepening, burning its one
   thought, exerting just
the same pressure on just
   the same spot.

Nothing by Halves

I picture them in a museum
       storeroom where clutter
has all but immobilized them both—
       the statuary
from ancient Chinese dynasties stands
       guard over (and more-
over, between) them: the exotic,
       echidnic, empty
suits of armor hunker in postures

of martial patience: impressionist
       paintings form pastel
labyrinths: pedestals impede them—
       and they are smashing
even the most impressive pieces
       without one morsel
of remorse, thrusting aside this vase
       and that last extant
example of Middle Kingdom glass

in their ungainly hunger to be
       against each other;
but they are only in their living
       room, raging, the air
humming like high-voltage power lines
       with their jealousies
and acidic contempt for themselves,
       and they are launching
immaterial artillery—

words they promised themselves they'd never
        pitch like dislodged bricks
in a back alley brawl, leaky Bics,
        the lesser china
they'd meant to donate to the thrift store
        anyway—and then
they graduate to the irreplace-
        able, the handmade
ceramics, sentimental gewgaws,

and obsolete bibelots now broken
        in a crescendo
of recrimination before they—
        no going back now—
move on to the big-ticket items
        (plasma-screen TV
tipped into oblivion, laptop
        cracked on the counter)
as if they would destroy anything

that might come between them, any balk
        in the obstacle
course of their love, as if the scattered
        fragments of their joined
lives were bright tesserae composing
        a mosaic fit
to glitter with their desire not just
        to have each other,
but to have each other completely.

Ode to Married Women

Dearests, whether once at a get-together
Tinted by a vintage from someone's vapor-
Barriered-and-climate-controlled wine cellar—
    Something to soften

Our resistance while we insisted nothing
Dangerous could happen—or over decades
Mackled with imagined amour, I've wondered
    Whether I wouldn't

Better cup the crease where your leg meets ass cheek,
Better know your nakedness through its newness,
Better set you quivering than that squibbish
    Husband who takes you

(This, I'd add, according to you) for granted—
Wondering, as well, should you chance to hear me
Sing of all your charms to myself, if you could
    Ever forgive me.

Nothing to be done, I suppose, and nothing
More for some poor rover like me to hope for,
But you understand why I sometimes archly
    Draw back in silence.

Here's the upshot, ladies: I never told you
Anything—the hand shock I suffered seeing
That ungodly ring, or the jolt of feeling
    Jealous your dry-loose

Hubby served as anchor and first-choice kisser
While he stroked your belly . . . I told you nothing.
Call me Saint Sebastian, a double martyr
    Prickling with Eros,

Praising the immutable with his mute girls
Healed into belief, but remember, dearests,
Love's an archer ready to use us both as
    Targets and arrows:

Now and then, I think about ways to win you,
Nocked and cocksure even the most enduring
Wedding band looks just like a bull's-eye, only
    Smaller and hollow.

Meant to Be

Cracked acorns punctuate the ground
Like grief, their scattered caps the cups
Rain overfills with chattering drops
That are themselves what they propound.

My lapsang souchong tastes like smoke.
I watch the low, collapsing sky
Collect in pools stained brown like whisky,
And dream of endless stands of oak,

Grand emblems of entelechy,
That realm where promised primrose blooms
And brushwood fuels the brisk, hushed flames
That flicker through my achy tea.

You're back. The courtyard sidewalk pops
With raindrops' goose bumps as you call
Up to my window, *It was all
A big mistake*. You stir my hopes:

*Our breaking up? Not that. Your life.
You made your grail a girl, a maid
Of High Romance, a fancy played
Up version of the perfect wife,*

*One no less hokey than the virgin
Volcano-bound in jungle flicks:
Priests pour libations, white fire licks
Her feet, Sir Rescue will emerge in*

*The nick of time, and presto!—lookie
Here!—Hero sweeps the sweatless girl
Right off the sacrificial grill
And into bliss! Now, ain't she lucky?*

Well spoken. Love was never meant
To be that easy, nor that scenic—
No wide shot of the oceanic
Cruise home to "Moonlight in Vermont"—

But mostly rain and smoke and doubt.
Tea's cold, dream's scuttled. In its wake,
I hear wild drumming. Chants. I take
My flooded heart and pour it out.

When I Don't Know What to Call This

Flowers I can't name
bloom in a pink profusion
namelessly complete—

if I say *petal*, what else have I done

but make each one one
and the same by giving them
one name? Flowering,

the tree itself has said it all already,

more eloquently,
the way our days together—
moment by moment—

once said themselves as perfectly as one

could ever wish time
to be said. That time now gone
without our having

discovered what to term this time apart—

minutes prolific
as leaf after greeny leaf—
I must come to trust

these days will say themselves as certainly

as petal or stem,
and that on some unknown one
soon, we'll find ourselves

daydreaming in the fallen ring of them.

Inedible Voice

I'm texting my beloved from nine thousand miles
away about last night's band (they let me sit in
on some easy changes), and I write, "The singer
    had the most inedible voice,"

then think, *Whoa, not what I meant*—in fact, it's nearly
the opposite, since his voice sounded as rich as dark
chocolate in dark chocolate sauce, I was eating it
    up all night long. We're doing this

long distance, my love and I, and though we're trying,
some days *that* feels inedible: the clustered texts,
the when-they-fit-in calls, the slackening silence
    after misinterpreted words.

Farewell, lips. Goodbye, gorgeous thighs. I remember
the last time I ate her out on the couch, her knees
cocked back, her legs bent like boomerangs, her face lost
    in what she was feeling, in what

I prayed, there on my knees, I was inviting her—
in the best way I know how—to feel, and it's less
that the memory's grown inedible somehow
    since I'm savoring it right now

and more that here, alone, in the distant present,
there's less to fill me up, I feel myself thinning,
wishing I were with that woman while she listens
    to a promising poet read

some intense, terse, sonically dense verses praising
the beneficent ravenousness of vultures,
each one of which is "the afterlife of all things"
    and "unzips sun-marinated

gristle from skin," and when she sent those lines, I sent
some where vultures are "dwarfed transfiguring angels"
and have, according to one version of mercy,
      "mercy enough to consume us

all and give us wings," and though these days I don't know
what to call whatever spreads the world before us—
God, the cosmos, fate, grace, fortune, the Great Spirit,
      or maybe just the world itself—

I keep praying the next thing it sets before me
to taste, taste and see, won't seem more inedible
tripe, some unfathomable mouthful, but rather
      what the world has meant all along

with everything I could get down if I'd open
my mouth and take it all ingenuously in—
rain, risk, the airy arabesques of the script in
      the clear book only she can read,

the white bookmark in the book we never finished,
her always ("When I sip coffee, fluff my pillow,
run my fingers against a brick wall . . .") my always,
      the whole blameworthy Pacific

ocean, the small lighthouse tattoo on her left thigh
calling me home, those gospel changes, the standing
ovation, the words we share, my fingers in her hair
      when they were in her hair, the two

missing letters, knob and hinge, I now can see are
a doorway, distance, grief, our loving each other
in spite of them—what I hope the world always means:
      here is something incredible.

Through Separation, Things Become Themselves

Eheu fugaces, Postume, Postume,
labuntur anni…

— Horace

In that first molten moment of compression,
Incomparable and dense with elements
That weren't yet elements, the unexplained
      Mother of all events
Occurred and gave the universe expression:
Of that explosion, matter's what remained.

We, too, began in mystery and heat
And now subside to distance, time, and friction.
Loss is our oldest language. Can I place
      Faith in that valediction
That called souls "gold to airy thinness beat"?
It's hard to face such thoughts without a face.

I'm frightened, love. The universe grew cold
And thereby more distinct. As space appears,
Will you grow weary of my quirks and charms?
      These aren't unfounded fears
To harbor here where spiral galaxies hold
Millions of empty light-years in their arms.

Part Fear, Part Mourning, Part Wild Melody

Beloved woman, beautiful and scared,
    My restless runner, self-fulfilled and thin,
I know despite how many I've prepared
    I'm running out of ways to call you in

From streets that echo with your footfalls' ache
    And settle into darkness so profound
On moonless nights that someone might mistake
    A pitfalled footpath for the safer ground.

What will I do when my invention fails
    And I, at last, must lean against the jamb
And picture you pursuing root-torn trails
    That carry you too far from where I am

For you to catch my voice, its complex note
    Part fear, part mourning, part wild melody,
Or hear the question catching in my throat:
    Why do you love your loneliness more than me?

Each Minute Rich with Infinite Potential

How often is
the temptation to claim
    a separation as
something large, a gorge
    or Grand Canyon,
a massive tectonic fault
    or deep-sea trench

    walled with basalt,
the rift by which
    a continent becomes
two and the two
    begin to drift,
when the greater devastations
    are the small—

    the missed good
night, the unmade call—
    each minute's minute
attrition the miniature fissure,
    the subatomic crack
from which whole cities
    never come back?

4

Something for Everything

Adam sat naming everything he'd miss.
　　　He couldn't quite explain
　　　Why he was doing this
Or how he drew such pleasure from the pain

Of his enumerations: snowdrops twice
　　　As vibrant from the view
　　　Outside of paradise,
And paradisiacal birds with curlicue

Tail feathers drooping in foreboding loops,
　　　And howler monkeys calling
　　　To other howler troops,
The shade trees and the footpaths and the falling

Fruit, unforbidden, he was meant to eat—
　　　To think of losing it
　　　Made every bite more sweet,
So he indulged such thinking as he bit,

Grateful that loss was merely nomenclature,
　　　A term to understand,
　　　And reveled in his nature
As Eve approached him, something in her hand.

Walking on the Beach, I Keep Noticing a Sunbather

Desire's the dime-sized aperture
Designed so only to admit
    The few things that will fit
Its strict dimensions, nothing more,

The way a door might have a slot
For one thin metal tray to clatter
    Through with its bread and butter—
No apple, pear, or apricot—

To feed a wretch who can't begin
To say what dire disease he's caught,
    That he should pray the slot
Stay narrow and the tray stay thin.

Define desire? A flint-hard glint
That burns the garden down to sighs.
    A narrowing of the eyes:
Cities contracted to a squint.

Desire's the way that suntan lotion
Dolloped and palmed along one knee
    Can imperceptibly
Obliterate the sunlit ocean.

"And All the Trees of the Field Shall Clap Their Hands"

The worshippers' raised arms
Almost arrhythmically
Swayed back and forth to more

Than music, deeper storms
Of desolate desire
Than those I must have heard,

The way the trees just now
Outside my window—gray,
Sun-struck, wind-winnowed—sway

Bough after leafless bough
In the cold winter air
Before the coming blizzard.

My Father's Father's Body

My grandpa built a go-cart out of junk:
An old lawnmower engine, scraps of metal,
A cupboard door, a cushion. The result
Was forty miles-per-hour of swerving joy—
Flung gravel, wind-snagged bugs, my father's arms
    Vined around mine to help me steer.
We gunned it past the neighbors' humdrum farms.
        The message: we are here.

Sometimes I think I thought of him as God,
Who teases out the mum petal by petal,
Who barks the trees and blades whole fields of grass,
Who skies the earth and sees the laughing boy
I was and loves him: clunkish, cloud-brained, his.
    A man all motor oil and steel
And most poetic in his silences,
        He made me something real.

Who didn't see the Lord's enduring blueprint?
Nightfall, dry riverbeds, the withered nettle.
He made it clear. Stage Four. Hemoptysis.
We had to watch the cancer cells destroy
My father's father's body, and the sight
    Told us what we'd need to know:
God takes the true mechanic's own delight
        In making something go.

Concerning Possibility

I am living at the edge of a new leaf.

— Arthur Sze

Petty to number every step unstepped,
The breaths unbreathed, the unremitting string
Of unexploded laughs and tears unwept,
    The un- of everything
    That by its nevering
Remains the only promise always kept . . .

Better to count the buds that braille the year,
Blossoms that offer their ambrosial shawl,
The bruised fruits that rescent the atmosphere
    Of summers past recall,
    And then to count the fall
Of every leaf that could have landed here,

Where you could be, sweet other that I lack,
Or you, or you—those picket gates clack shut—
Who never crackled down the spindly track
    Of mays and mights that cut
    Into the woods of what
A heaven, to be heaven, must give back.

The Only Cure

Wild, horsey sex after a couple of rounds
Of quick, flirtatious cocktails might sound right—
Hard to weigh losses when your headboard pounds
Against the wall, and weightlessness tonight
Is all you want—or a tooth-loosening fight,
A snapped-cue, broken-bottle shivaree
That channels spite into a brief respite.
Grief is the only cure for tragedy.

You thumb through *Kant for Dummies*, which confounds
Your sense of purpose and of prose despite
How comforting the introduction sounds.
You've always held yourself an erudite
Adult, yet now you realize how slight
Are the consolations of philosophy:
Debating pain's truth won't untooth its bite.
Grief is the only cure for tragedy.

You pen a dazzling ballad. Grace abounds,
And nuance; not a whit of blatherskite
About the pearly gates or golden grounds
Of heaven mars your work; it's watertight,
Which means you haven't wept. Although you might
Have hoped in blind-faith making, now you see
Art can survive as sorrow's parasite;
Grief is the only cure for tragedy.

The dust motes drifting through the morning light
Promise the one thing time can guarantee.
You grab a scrap sheet and, believing, write,
Grief is the only cure for tragedy.

Vehicle of Wonder

Forklifted down from distant shelves,
Shipped on a flatbed, it has come
Fully assembled for the new
Owners, who bear the tedium
Of being types the makers knew
Could not assemble it themselves.

It's bigger than they thought. They pry
Open and junk the wooden crate,
Then step inside and flip a switch.
It starts to shake. Lights scintillate
Symphonically till, glitch by glitch,
They flare and fizzle while the high

Pitched whines, metallic creaks, and grinding
Where gears meet other gears provoke
More puckered shame than anything.
They catch a whiff of awkward smoke.
It ratchets to a stop. They spring
The door and step into their blinding

Front yard. The owners can't deny
This part: the vehicle goes nowhere.
It doesn't wormhole them through space
Or time. The vehicle goes nowhere—
They're home, the most familiar place,
And one day both still have to die—

Yet on this brightest of afternoons,
They walk into their house and blink:
Oh, look, they say—their sectional,
A doorknob, rugs, the kitchen sink—
And murmur, *Aren't they beautiful,*
Viewing again their same old spoons.

"The Tyranny of the Present"

> It is as strange as if a fish
> were repeatedly surprised
> at the wetness of water.
>
> — C. S. Lewis

He handed me the present
Immaculately wrapped
In spangled, pale blue paper
That rippled as though rain
Were riveting a river,
And I could not explain
Why I felt set adrift
And, at the same time, trapped
By something like a gift.

I tensed with hesitation—
Only because I know
How often gratitude,
For all its good, is tied
With the imperfect bow
Of future obligation—
And clutched my present, shy,
My heart a little swift
And mouth a little dry.

I pulled the bow, surprised
It didn't stick, then tore
The paper off, unsnapped
A box's latch, and raised
Its wooden lid. He sighed.
A grin appeared like water
From under a closed door
Spreading across the floor.
There was nothing inside.

A moment, he intoned,
I've given you a moment,
And what grace more sublime—
What kinder end intend
As minutes pour through years—
Than that I have this time,
The medium I live in,
A gift that disappears
The moment it is given?

Sabine Jars

Fleet-featured, famished, sweet, your date appears
For canapés and cocktail-tinctured tales
While candle flames' flamboyant press-on nails
Point ceilingward where pristine chandeliers
Seem frozen orreries composed of tears,
And soon the feast arrives, and language fails
To paint how suddenly the evening pales,
The meal is gone—as swiftly as the years—
And now you realize this was your life,
This interlude of badinage and food,
And you accept with tasteful gratitude
(As keen, as poignant, as your napkinned knife)
Your feeling full, although when you were younger
This hardly would have satisfied your hunger.

Reading Thomas Merton in *Le déjeuner des canotiers*

Our mind swims in the air of an understanding, a reality that is dark
and serene and includes in itself everything. Nothing more is desired.

— Thomas Merton

This yawning, lush, mimosa atmosphere
     Has soaked us in the clear
Knowledge we have, at last, surpassed desire
     And need no more aspire
To better standings nor more understanding—
     We're done with all demanding,
All lesser satisfactions, and have grown
     Into a known unknown;
Enlightened in that dark, we feel serene
     And take this air to mean
All's well. The lavish pastel pinks and peaches
     That flush our furthest reaches
Compose such plushly poignant scenes, we're far
     Beyond the brush Renoir
Once used to paint us. It's as if we sat in
     Our own small boats of satin
And drifted down the cold, ash-colored river
     Of nowhere and forever.

Meant, in Time, to Crack

I count the seconds, click by weighted click,
As though they were the tumblers to a safe
    I meant, in time, to crack,

Knowing that if it took a hundred years
Of nimble-fingered tuning and retuning
    And a musician's ears

To learn the art—a lifetime spent in straining
To hear that moment when the moment catches—
    It would be worth the training

To watch the most unlikely door swing wide
As I breathe deep and reach into the darkness
    To touch what waits inside.

What the Rain Says

Because the night is warm, a warm
Rain drones the score it must perform,
Each drop a sole self, yet those drops
    All part of the same storm
      That never stops,

Intoning something we might hear
As countless voices brought to cheer
Or, through some upstart artifice,
    To gasp at once with fear,
      To sigh or hiss

In concert as each consort blends
Into the air that never ends,
A counterpoint of throes and threnes,
    Some music that portends
      What all this means—

But through the drowsy, half-doused hush,
The raindrops in their descants rush
To sound out their determined calling,
    The patient bedtime *shush*
      They make by falling.

Notes

"Tropical Cyclones Help to Maintain Equilibrium in the Earth's Troposphere, and to Maintain a Relatively Stable and Warm Temperature Worldwide": The title comes from a previous incarnation of the Wikipedia entry on tropical cyclones. This language no longer appears there.

Immaterial Witness: Certain details in this poem are drawn from *Seducing the Subconscious: The Psychology of Emotional Influence in Advertising* by Robert Heath.

We Have Agreed: The epigraph by Keats comes from "Ode on a Grecian Urn."

Inedible Voice: The first quoted poet is Sarah Holland-Batt and the poem, "The Vulture"; the second quoted poet is David Bottoms and the poem, "Under the Vulture-Tree."

Through Separation, Things Become Themselves: The epigraph by Horace comes from the *Odes* (II.xiv) and reads, in James Michie's excellent translation, "Ah, how they glide by, Postumus, Postumus, / The years, the swift years!"

"And All the Trees of the Field Shall Clap Their Hands": The title comes from Isaiah 55:12 (KJV).

Concerning Possibility: The epigraph by Arthur Sze comes from "The Shapes of Leaves."

"The Tyranny of the Present": Although the title phrase appears in a variety of places, I believe I took note of it in John Polkinhorne's *The God of Hope and the End of the World*. (I should take better notes.) The epigraph by C.S. Lewis comes from *Reflections on the Psalms*, but I suspect I encountered it in Philip Yancey's *Disappointment with God*.

Reading Thomas Merton in *Le déjeuner des canotiers*: The epigraph by Thomas Merton comes from *New Seeds of Contemplation*.

A Note About the Author

Stephen Kampa was born in Missoula, Montana, and raised in Daytona Beach, Florida. He holds degrees from Carleton College and Johns Hopkins University. His previous books are *Cracks in the Invisible* (Ohio University Press, 2011), which won both the Hollis Summers Poetry Prize and the Gold Medal in Poetry from the Florida Book Awards, and *Bachelor Pad* (Waywiser, 2014). His session work can be heard on Robert "Top" Thomas's *The Town Crier* (WildRoot Records) and Victor Wainwright's *Boom Town* (Blind Pig Records). He teaches at Flagler College.

Other Books from Waywiser

Other Books from Waywiser

W. D. Snodgrass, *Not for Specialists: New & Selected Poems*
Mark Strand, *Almost Invisible*
Mark Strand, *Blizzard of One*
Bradford Gray Telford, *Perfect Hurt*
Matthew Thorburn, *This Time Tomorrow*
Cody Walker, *Shuffle and Breakdown*
Cody Walker, *The Self-Styled No-Child*
Cody Walker, *The Trumpiad*
Deborah Warren, *The Size of Happiness*
Clive Watkins, *Already the Flames*
Clive Watkins, *Jigsaw*
Mike White, *Addendum to a Miracle*
Richard Wilbur, *Anterooms*
Richard Wilbur, *Mayflies*
Richard Wilbur, *Collected Poems 1943-2004*
Norman Williams, *One Unblinking Eye*
Greg Williamson, *A Most Marvelous Piece of Luck*
Greg Williamson, *The Hole Story of Kirby the Sneak and Arlo the True*
Stephen Yenser, *Stone Fruit*

FICTION
Gregory Heath, *The Entire Animal*
Mary Elizabeth Pope, *Divining Venus*
K. M. Ross, *The Blinding Walk*
Gabriel Roth, *The Unknowns**
Matthew Yorke, *Chancing It*

ILLUSTRATED
Nicholas Garland, *I wish ...*
Eric McHenry and Nicholas Garland, *Mommy Daddy Evan Sage*
Greg Williamson, *The Hole Story of Kirby the Sneak and Arlo the True*

NON-FICTION
Neil Berry, *Articles of Faith: The Story of British Intellectual Journalism*
Mark Ford, *A Driftwood Altar: Essays and Reviews*
Philip Hoy, ed., *A Bountiful Harvest:*
The Correspondence of Anthony Hecht and William L. MacDonald
Richard Wollheim, *Germs: A Memoir of Childhood*

* Co-published with Picador